IT SERVICE MANAGEMENT FOUNDATION QUESTIONS
For ITIL® v3 foundation
exam candidate

Sheffield Hallam University
Learning and IT Services
Adsetts Centre City Campus
Sheffield S1 1WB

101 942 224 6

D0121303

Sheffield Hallam
University
WITHDRAWN

BCS The Chartered Institute for IT

BCS The Chartered Institute for IT promotes wider social and economic progress through the advancement of information technology, science and practice. We bring together industry, academics, practitioners and government to share knowledge, promote new thinking, inform the design of new curricula, shape public policy and inform the public. As the professional membership and accreditation body for IT, we serve over 70,000 members including practitioners, academics and students, in the UK and internationally. A leading IT qualification body, we offer a range of widely recognised professional and end-user qualifications.

JOINING BCS

BCS qualifications, products and services are designed with your career plans in mind. We not only provide essential recognition through professional qualifications but also offer many other useful benefits to our members at every level.

BCS Membership demonstrates your commitment to professional development. It helps to set you apart from other IT practitioners and provides industry recognition of your skills and experience. Employers and customers increasingly require proof of professional qualifications and competence. Professional membership confirms your competence and integrity and sets an independent standard that people can trust. Professional Membership (MBCS) is the pathway to Chartered IT Professional (CITP) Status.
www.bcs.org/membership

Further Information
BCS The Chartered Institute for IT, First Floor, Block D, North Star House, North Star Avenue, Swindon SN2 1FA, United Kingdom
T +44 (0) 1793 417 424
F +44 (0) 1793 417 444
www.bcs.org/contact

IT SERVICE MANAGEMENT FOUNDATION PRACTICE QUESTIONS
For ITIL® v3 foundation exam candidates

Steve Mann (Editor), Tony Gannon, Nigel Mear

© 2009 British Informatics Society Limited

All rights reserved. Apart from any fair dealing for the purposes of research or private study, or criticism or review, as permitted by the Copyright Designs and Patents Act 1988, no part of this publication may be reproduced, stored or transmitted in any form or by any means, except with the prior permission in writing of the publisher, or in the case of reprographic reproduction, in accordance with the terms of the licences issued by the Copyright Licensing Agency. Enquiries for permission to reproduce material outside those terms should be directed to the publisher.

All trade marks, registered names etc. acknowledged in this publication are the property of their respective owners. BCS and the BCS logo are the registered trade marks of the British Computer Society charity number 292786 (BCS).

ITIL® – "ITIL® is a Registered Trade Mark of the Office of Government Commerce in the United Kingdom and other countries."

Published by British Informatics Society Limited (BISL), a wholly owned subsidiary of BCS
The Chartered Institute for IT, First Floor, Block D, North Star House, North Star Avenue,
Swindon, SN2 1FA, United Kingdom.
www.bcs.org

ISBN 978-1-906124-18-2

British Cataloguing in Publication Data.
A CIP catalogue record for this book is available at the British Library.

Disclaimer:
The views expressed in this book are of the author(s) and do not necessarily reflect the views of BISL or BCS except where explicitly stated as such.

Although every care has been taken by the authors and BISL in the preparation of the publication, no warranty is given by the authors or BISL as publisher as to the accuracy or completeness of the information contained within it and neither the authors nor BISL shall be responsible or liable for any loss or damage whatsoever arising by virtue of such information or any instructions or advice contained within this publication or by any of the aforementioned.

Typeset by Lapiz Digital Services, Chennai, India.
Printed at CPI Antony Rowe, Chippenham, UK.

CONTENTS

AUTHORS

Steve Mann has spent over 30 years in IT Service Management following a number of roles in IT Operations. He worked for ICL as Operations Manager at the European Union in Luxembourg from 1979 to 1982, then as Operations and Production Manager for the Abu Dhabi National Oil Company (ADNOC) in the UAE before returning to the UK to work for BREL (British Rail Engineering Limited), where he project-managed mainframe installations, Leeds & Holbeck Building Society, where he first met and introduced ITIL®, followed by training and consultancy roles with SYSOP in Rochdale. In 2001, Steve created his own company, SM2 Ltd, and offers Service Management training, consultancy and coaching using both ITIL and ISO 20000 as a basis. SM2 works very closely with a Belgian society, OPSYS and together as 'Opsys-sm2' offer accredited ITIL and ISO 20000 training in various locations around the world.

Tony Gannon began his IT career in 1985 on leaving HM Forces and has been active in the ITSM industry since then. Tony has previously contributed to ITSM publications, is a regular at Service Management events and was previously itSMF Northern Regional Chair. He has helped organisations to implement, better understand, or improve their ITSM capability for over 15 years. Tony understands fully the sometimes painful process of dealing with the hype and the reality when implementing a professional ITSM practice. He adopts a 'lean' and pragmatic approach to interpreting ITIL guidance into workable solutions.

Nigel Mear has been involved in Service Management for nearly 25 years and has worked for organisations including the BBC, IBM, BT, and C&W. Early in his career he took an interest in performance, learning and development and is now an accomplished consultant, trainer and professionally accredited business coach, working with teams and individuals at all levels. He is director of Solid Air Consultancy Ltd, providing specialist training and coaching services to Service Management teams and organisations. He is an active member of BCS, Institute of IT Service Management, European Mentoring & Coaching Council, itSMF and Association for Coaching.

ITIL® – "ITIL® is a Registered Trade Mark of the Office of Government Commerce in the United Kingdom and other countries."

INTRODUCTION

The purpose of this book is to help students understand how to address multiple-choice examination questions related to IT Service Management at Foundation level.

The book covers examination question types, hints and tips for success, and examples of typical questions in each of the Service Management Lifecycle phases.

It is assumed that the reader will have either attended a Foundation course, followed a self-study approach and/or have relevant Service Management experience. This book is neither a mini-guide to Service Management nor a 'short course'.

The book presents Service Management questions as they would be encountered in an ITIL Service Management Foundation Examination. It is an excellent way of revising before an examination because it covers the learning areas needed to be understood and presents them as they will be seen in an examination.

For ease of use, this book is structured around the Service Lifecycle.

A companion book, *IT Service Management – A Guide for ITIL® v3 Foundation Exam Candidates*, which provides students with a study guide covering the key topics relevant to these questions, is available from BCS.

Throughout the book, the portions of text indicated by the use of quotation marks and a † symbol have been taken directly from the OGC ITIL Framework publications:

Service Strategy. ISBN: 9780113310456
Service Design. ISBN: 9780113310470
Service Transition. ISBN: 9780113310487
Service Operation. ISBN: 9780113310463
Continual Service Improvement. ISBN: 9780113310494

© Crown copyright material is reproduced with the permission of the Controller of HMSO and Queen's Printer for Scotland.

SECTION 1:
EXAMINATION AND QUESTION TYPES

1   SERVICE MANAGEMENT EXAMINATION

It is highly recommended that students attend an accredited training course before attempting the ITIL Foundation Examination. Training providers will make arrangements for students to sit the examination, typically at the end of the three-day course. Attending a course is the best way for you to be prepared for your examination, and to gain a fuller comprehension of Service Management.

The Official Accreditor has the responsibility of setting the syllabus for the ITIL Foundation Examination. The syllabus is liable to updates from time to time, so students should ensure they are aware of the current version. The Official Accreditor is appointed by the Office of Government Commerce (OGC), who is responsible for ITIL v3. At the time of writing the Official Accreditor is the APMGroup.

Examinations are provided by accredited Examination Institutes (EIs), such as the Information Systems Examination Board (ISEB), which is part of the British Computer Society (BCS).

THE BASICS OF THE EXAMINATION

- An ITIL Service Management examination consists of 40 multiple-choice questions.
- English-speaking students have 60 minutes to complete the paper.
- The pass mark is 65% (26/40).
- There are always four 'response alternatives': A, B, C, D.
- Only one answer is correct per question.
- No marks are deducted if a wrong answer is given (i.e. there is no 'negative marking').

The examination papers are designed to cover the whole topic of Service Management in proportion to the prescribed weightings in the official syllabus. This ensures there will be a wide spread of questions on each paper and that the papers will be well balanced.

The official ITIL Foundation syllabus can be found on the BCS/ISEB website.

2   MULTIPLE-CHOICE QUESTIONS

We will now look at the question anatomy and the different types of question in the ITIL Service Management Examination.

ANATOMY OF A MULTIPLE-CHOICE QUESTION

A multiple-choice question comprises two main parts: the 'stem' and the 'response alternatives'.

The stem is 'the question' and the 'response alternatives' are the potential answers. Incorrect responses are known as 'distracters'. A set of good distracters makes a question harder than one with poor distracters.

> **HINT**
>
> Read the question and all the response alternatives at least twice before deciding on your answer.

Here are some examples. The answers to the questions used as examples can be found at the end of this chapter on page 10.

> **EXAMPLE 1**
>
> **Stem**
> How many phases are there in the Service Lifecycle?
>
> **Response alternatives**
> A   6
> B   5
> C   4
> D   3

Simply pick the right answer!

Some questions will not follow the simple approach of Example 1. An alternative style, very common in Service Management examinations, is to list 'statements', and then offer a selection of response alternatives.

EXAMPLE 2

Stem
Which of the following are reasons for investing in Service Management?

Statements
1 Increased customer satisfaction
2 Increased levels of availability
3 Reduction in the number of Incidents
4 Increased number of SLA breaches

Response alternatives
A 1, 2 and 3 only
B 1, 2 and 4 only
C 1, 3 and 4 only
D 2, 3 and 4 only

In questions like Example 2, you need to look at each statement and decide if it meets the criteria in the 'stem'. In the example, does the statement give a good reason for investing in Service Management? If you feel it does, include the statement, if not exclude it.

HINT

There are two ways of approaching the 'list' type of question.

One way is to look at the statements to see which are 'positive' (i.e. those that meet the requirement of the question) and select the appropriate response.

An alternative way is to identify which statement is 'negative' and select the response that does **not** include that statement.

Combining these approaches provides a 'quality check' of your answer.

TYPES OF MULTIPLE-CHOICE QUESTION

There are many different types of multiple-choice question. Here are a few examples of the different types of question you may encounter.

Standard

The 'standard' question is a simple 'stem' with four 'response alternatives'. A typical examination paper will have more 'standard' questions than other types. Standard questions are considered less confusing to answer than the other types of question, and they are (usually) shorter.

EXAMPLE 3

How many main functional areas are described in the Service Operation lifecycle phase?

A 6
B 5
C 4
D 3

As we have already seen, simply choose the correct answer.

Standard negative

The 'standard' question above could be referred to as 'standard positive'. Another type of question is known as 'standard negative'. This is where the 'stem' contains a negative word such as NOT or LEAST.

In 'standard negative' questions, the negative word is usually printed in CAPITALS.

EXAMPLE 4

Which of the following pieces of data is LEAST useful when diagnosing an Incident?

A The identity of the user who called the Service Desk to report the Incident
B The cost of the CI that is affected by the Incident
C The unique identity of the affected CI
D The time and date the Incident was reported

Again, simply pick the correct answer.

HINT

A common mistake is to miss the negative word in the stem. If you read through the paper too quickly you potentially risk losing marks.

Standard definition or matching

A variation of the standard question is where the subject is a definition and you have to 'match' the definition to the correct description. This is often referred to as a 'standard definition' or 'matching' question.

EXAMPLE 5

Which of the following is the best definition of an Incident?

A   A warning that a threshold has been reached, something has changed, or a failure has occurred
B   The addition, modification or removal of anything that could have an effect on IT Services
C   An unplanned interruption to an IT Service, reduction in the quality of an IT Service or the failure of a Configuration Item that has not yet affected Service
D   The unknown cause of one or more Incidents

HINT

A definition question is a 'gift' – providing you know the definition! All four response alternatives in Example 5 are Service Management ITIL definitions. In some questions the distracters (the incorrect responses) may not be real Service Management definitions.

List

A 'list' question is where a list of statements is given and you are required to select those that satisfy the criteria proposed in the 'stem'.

EXAMPLE 6

Which of the following actions are included in the Event Management process?

1   Generation
2   Detection
3   Filtered
4   Correction
5   Closure

A   1, 2, 3 and 4 only
B   2, 3, 4 and 5 only
C   1, 2, 3 and 5 only
D   1, 3, 4 and 5 only

The question in Example 6 uses the Event Management process. One of the actions is incorrect (see the answer on page 10 for which one). There are two ways of arriving at the right answer (for each one, you need to know the process!):

- If you can identify the incorrect action, choose the option where that action is not included.

- Alternatively work through the options until you find the answer with the four correct actions.

Matching columns

A 'matching columns' question presents you with two lists. You have to 'match' an item in column B with a statement in column A. Here's an example to illustrate how it works.

EXAMPLE 7

Match the lifecycle process in column B with the correct lifecycle phase in column A.

	Column A		Column B
1	Service Strategy	w	Capacity Management
2	Service Design	x	Demand Management
3	Service Transition	y	Event Management
4	Service Operation	z	Knowledge Management

A	1 w	2 y	3 x	4 z
B	1 x	2 w	3 z	4 y
C	1 z	2 x	3 y	4 w
D	1 y	2 z	3 w	4 x

This is a simplified example as the items in both columns appear only once in each 'response alternative'. Also, because each possible 'matching' appears only once within the response alternatives, as soon as you have identified one correct matching pair you have the correct answer.

For example if you think Service Operation ('4' in column A) is where you would find Event Management ('y' in column B) you would choose option 'B' because it is the only one which includes '4 y'. Again, there are two ways of arriving at the correct answer: you can identify the correct pairings as above, or you can identify incorrect pairings to eliminate false options.

A further note on 'distracters'

The following will help you understand and prepare to deal with distracters (i.e. the wrong 'response alternatives'). Sometimes a distracter will be completely incorrect, however, there will be times when a distracter will contain some elements of truth.

Some questions will require you to make a judgement to determine which response alternative is the 'best' response to the question posed in the stem. Variations on this style of question can require you to select the 'least', 'most', 'main', response etc.

It is good practice to highlight the words 'best', 'least' etc. in the stem and then, for this style of question, carefully read all the response alternatives and use your judgement to select the most appropriate option based on the relative strength of the proposition in relation to ITIL guidance, and the specific question being asked.

Here's an example.

EXAMPLE 8

Which of the following best describes 'ITIL' Service Management?

A   A set of books
B   Five books together with some complementary 'guidance'
C   A Service Management publication
D   Service Management guidance based on 'best practice'

All the response alternatives are 'true', however, one is best (i.e. it is more complete, more accurate, more appropriate etc.). Which is it?

Summary
The question types above are the main types of question you should encounter in an ITIL Service Management Foundation Examination.

You may notice as you work through the questions that different styles of writing have been used in creating the questions. This is deliberate. Foundation Examination paper questions are written by a group of authors over a period of time, and we have reflected this in this publication. Consequently, there will be variations in the style of language and phrasing used.

And now for the answers to the example questions.

ANSWERS TO EXAMPLES IN CHAPTER 2

Anatomy of a multiple-choice question

Example 1
B There are five phases within the ITIL v3 lifecycle: Service Strategy, Service Design, Service Transition, Service Operation and Continual Service Improvement.

Example 2
A Increasing the number of SLA breaches is not a reason (a benefit) to invest in Service Management. The other statements are all good reasons to invest in Service Management.

Types of multiple-choice question

Example 3 (standard)
C There are four main functional areas described within Service Operations: Service Desk, Technical Management, Application Management and IT Operations Management.

Example 4 (standard negative)
B The cost of a CI is least relevant when resolving an Incident as the cost does not impact on the performance of a CI. The other data is essential in managing the Incident effectively and restoring service as soon as possible.

Example 5 (standard definition)
C This is the correct definition of an Incident. The other options are ITIL definitions of an Alert (A), a Change (B) and a Problem (D).

Example 6 (list)
C The action 'Correction' is incorrect – it should be 'Correlation'.

Example 7 (matching columns)
B The correct combinations are SS–Demand Management, SD–Capacity Management, ST–Knowledge Management and SO–Event Management.

Example 8 (distracters)
D This is the most complete, most accurate and most appropriate option.

SECTION 2:
FOUNDATION PRACTICE QUESTIONS

This section contains a comprehensive range of questions from across the ITIL Service Management Foundation syllabus covering all aspects of the lifecycle and Service Management principles in general. It is structured to follow a chronological order through the lifecycle of Service Management:

- Service Management as a practice
- The Service Lifecycle
- Service Strategy
- Service Design
- Service Transition
- Service Operation
- Functions
- Continual Service Improvement
- Processes
- Technology and Architecture
- Sample questions from across the lifecycle

The chapter or section reference after a question refers to the location in the companion book, *IT Service Management A Guide for ITIL® v3 Foundation Exam Candidates*, where the topic of the question is covered.

3 SERVICE MANAGEMENT AS A PRACTICE

The answers to questions in this chapter are on page 16.

SM 01

There are several sources of good practice including public frameworks, standards, and the proprietary knowledge of organisations and individuals.

Which of the following statements are correct?

1 Proprietary knowledge is difficult to replicate or transfer
2 Standards are only available through licensing agreements
3 Organisations should cultivate their own proprietary knowledge
4 Public frameworks are validated across multiple organisations

A 1 and 4 only
B 1, 2 and 3 only
C 2, 3 and 4 only
D 1, 3 and 4 only

See Guide Chapter 1

SM 02

Which of the following best describes how services deliver value to customers?

A Enabling the effective outsourcing of IT Services
B Reducing the overall cost of IT Service provision
C Facilitating the outcomes customers want to achieve
D Ensuring successful project delivery to the business

See Guide Chapter 1

SM 03

ITIL has become the most widely accepted approach to Service Management in the world. Which of the following is INCORRECT about Service Management?

A   Service Management is a professional practice supported by an extensive body of knowledge

B   Service Management is a set of specialised organisational capabilities for providing value to customers

C   Adoption of Service Management has grown primarily due to advances in tools and technology

D   Formal schemes exist for education, training and certification in Service Management

See Guide Chapter 1

SM 04

Match the definition from column A with the correct concept in column B.

	Column A		Column B
1	A means of delivering value to customers by facilitating outcomes customers want to achieve without the ownership of specific costs and risks	w	A service
2	A set of specialised organisational capabilities for providing value to customers in the form of services	x	A role
3	A team or group of people and the tools they use to carry out one or more processes or activities	y	Service Management
4	A set of responsibilities, activities and authorities granted to a person or team	z	A function

A   1 w   2 y   3 z   4 x
B   1 w   2 x   3 z   4 y
C   1 y   2 z   3 x   4 w
D   1 y   2 z   3 w   4 x

See Guide Chapter 1

SM 05

Which of the following statements are correct?

1   Functions are specialised to perform certain types of work
2   Functions accumulate their own body of knowledge through experience
3   Functions improve coordination through developing their own processes
4   Functions provide structure and stability to organisations

A   1 and 2 only
B   1 and 4 only
C   2, 3 and 4 only
D   1, 2 and 4 only

See Guide Chapter 1

ANSWERS TO 'SERVICE MANAGEMENT AS A PRACTICE' QUESTIONS

SM 01
D Statement 2 is incorrect. Frameworks and standards are publicly available and not available only through licensing agreements. The other statements all correctly describe good practice.

SM 02
C "A service delivers value to customers by facilitating outcomes customers want to achieve without the ownership of specific costs and risks."† This is the ITIL definition of a Service.

SM 03
C Service Management tools are essential for effective Service Management, however, it is incorrect to state that the adoption of Service Management has grown primarily due to advances in tools and technology.

SM 04
A These are standard ITIL Service Management definitions.

SM 05
D Statement 3 is incorrect. If functions develop their own processes, then this can potentially lead to functional silos that hinder coordination and alignment across functional areas. Coordination between functions through well-defined shared processes can improve productivity within and across functions.

4 THE SERVICE LIFECYCLE

The answers to questions in this chapter are on page 21.

SL 01

From the customer viewpoint, in which phase of the lifecycle is actual value seen?

A Service Strategy
B Service Design
C Service Transition
D Service Operation

See Guide Section 2

SL 02

Which phases of the Service Lifecycle are known as the 'progressive phases'?

A Service Strategy and Continual Service Improvement
B All five of the lifecycle phases
C None of the lifecycle phases
D Service Design, Service Transition and Service Operation

See Guide Section 2

SL 03

Which phase of the lifecycle provides guidance on managing complexities associated with changes to services involving Release Management, Programme Management and Risk Management?

A Service Design
B Service Operation
C Service Strategy
D Service Transition

See Guide Section 2

SL 04

Which of the following statements best describe Utility and Warranty from the customer's perspective?

A   A measure of how the service is delivered
B   An outcome-based definition of services
C   The two primary elements of value composition
D   A description of what the supplier wants to provide

See Guide Chapter 2

SL 05

What distinctive 'capabilities' do service providers need to develop?

A   Management, Information, Processes, Organisation, Infrastructure
B   Management, Applications, Information, Knowledge, People
C   Management, Knowledge, Processes, Organisation, People
D   Management, Knowledge, Information, Organisation, People

See Guide Chapter 2

SL 06

For which phase of the Service Lifecycle is it most important to take a holistic approach?

A   Service Strategy
B   Service Design
C   Service Transition
D   Service Operation

See Guide Section 2

SL 07

Which of the following is NOT a direct benefit that will come from the Service Design phase of the lifecycle?

A   Timely cancellation or changes to maintenance contracts for hardware and software when components are disposed of or decommissioned
B   Reduced total costs of ownership
C   Improved IT Governance with the identification and communication of a set of controls for effective governance of IT
D   More effective service performance with incorporation and recognition of Capacity, Availability and IT Continuity Plans

See Guide Chapter 3

SL 08

The ITIL framework provides a source of good practice in Service Management. Which of the following statements about ITIL are correct?

1   The core ITIL publications are applicable to all types of organisations
2   The structure of the ITIL core is in the form of a process framework
3   ITIL provides complementary guidance for specific industry sectors
4   ITIL can be adapted for use in various business environments

A   1 and 2 only
B   2 and 4 only
C   1, 3 and 4 only
D   1, 2 and 4 only

See Guide Chapter 1

SL 09

In which core publication are Change Management and Knowledge Management detailed?

A   Service Design
B   Service Operation
C   Service Strategy
D   Service Transition

See Guide Section 2

SL 10

Demand Management interfaces very closely with, and has a dependency on, which other process?

A   Capacity Management
B   Availability Management
C   Change Management
D   Service Portfolio Management

See Guide Chapter 8

SL 11

Output from Service Strategy is used as input to plan new and changed services in which phase of the Service Lifecycle?

A Service Design
B Service Operation
C Service Strategy
D Service Transition

See Guide Chapter 2

SL 12

Which of the following is NOT a goal or an objective of Service Design?

A Designing effective and efficient processes to manage services throughout their lifecycle
B Identifying and managing risks
C Designing remediation plans to cater for failed implementations
D Producing IT plans, processes and policies to provide quality IT solutions

See Guide Chapter 3

ANSWERS TO 'SERVICE LIFECYCLE' QUESTIONS

SL 01
D Service Operation is where the value (benefit) of a service is actually visible to the customer (it delivers the service to the customer) and the 'value captured' (the return from delivering the service) is available to the provider.

SL 02
D Three of the lifecycle phases are referred to as 'progressive phases' (SD, ST, SO). The other two are referred to as 'ongoing' phases (SS, CSI).

SL 03
D Service Transition has the objective of successfully managing all aspects of service changes within the predicted cost, quality and time estimates.

SL 04
C From the customer's perspective, value consists of two primary elements: Utility or 'fitness for purpose', and Warranty or 'fitness for use'. Option A refers to warranty, Options B and D do not refer specifically to utility or warranty.

SL 05
C Management, Knowledge, Processes, Organisation and People are all capabilities that need to be developed over time. Information, Infrastructure and Applications are resources and not capabilities. "Capabilities represent an organisation's ability to coordinate, control and deploy resources to produce value."† Capabilities differentiate service providers.

SL 06
B It is important that a holistic approach to all aspects of design is adopted. This will ensure not only that the functional elements are addressed by the design, but also that all of the management and operational requirements are addressed as a fundamental part of design.

SL 07
A Option A is a benefit that can be realised from Service Transition (and in some cases Service Operation) by good transition planning (taking away 'old' CIs). Options B, C and D are all benefits that should be provided by good Service Design.

SL 08
C Statement 2 is incorrect. The structure of the ITIL Core is in the form of a Service Lifecycle and not a process framework.

SL 09
D Change Management and Knowledge Management are detailed in Service Transition. Both these processes are critical during the Transition stage but influence and support all lifecycle phases.

SL 10

A Capacity Management interfaces very closely with Demand Management. A key activity within Demand Management is understanding Patterns of Business Activity (PBAs) to provide a sufficient basis for provision of capacity to meet these demands.

SL 11

A Service Design converts strategic objectives into portfolios of services and service assets.

SL 12

C Service Transition is responsible for remediation planning to cater for a failed change implementation.

5 SERVICE STRATEGY

The answers to questions in this chapter are on page 28.

SS 01

Which of the following describes the main way in which the Service Strategy publication can assist an organisation?

A   To manage strategic relationships within the IT industry
B   To implement ITIL within an IT organisation
C   To enable strategic integration with customers and suppliers
D   To develop Service Management as a strategic asset

See Guide Chapter 2

SS 02

Which of the following statements about the Service Portfolio are correct?

1   The Service Portfolio represents the investments made by a service provider
2   The Service Portfolio includes third party services that are part of service offerings
3   The Service Portfolio represents the ability of a service provider to serve customers and market spaces

A   1 and 2 only
B   All of the above
C   1 and 3 only
D   2 and 3 only

See Guide Chapter 2
See Guide Chapter 9

SS 03

What details are contained in the Service Pipeline?

A Operational capability within the context of a market space
B The resources engaged in all phases of the Service Lifecycle
C Business requirements that have not yet become live services
D Knowledge and information about phased-out services

See Guide Chapter 9

SS 04

Which of the following statements is/are correct about IT Governance?

1 IT Governance is an integral part of enterprise governance
2 IT Governance is the responsibility of the board of directors
3 IT Governance enables organisations to benchmark processes

A 1 only
B 1 and 2 only
C 2 and 3 only
D All of the above

See Guide Chapter 2

SS 05

A Business Case can be most accurately described as?

A A method for tracking business expenditure
B A decision support and planning tool
C A management tool for business communication
D A technique for calculating service valuation

See Guide Chapter 7

SS 06

From a Service Management perspective which of the following is NOT a specific risk management activity?

A Financial analysis of the likely consequences of a business action
B Ensuring processes are in place for ongoing monitoring of risks
C Identification and selection of appropriate countermeasures
D Having access to reliable and up-to-date information about risks

SS 07

It is important to distinguish between the three different types of service provider. Which of the following most accurately describes the main difference between Type I and Type II service providers?

A   Type I providers are internal and Type II provide external services
B   Type I providers are internal and Type II provide shared services
C   Type I providers are external and Type II provide internal services
D   Type I providers are technology focused and Type II business focused

See Guide Chapter 2

SS 08

Value is defined not only in terms of the customer's business outcomes, it is also highly dependent on?

A   The maturity of the IT processes
B   Managing the cost of service provision
C   The customer's perceptions
D   Effective resource utilisation

See Guide Chapter 2

SS 09

Which of the following most accurately describes the need for service providers to develop a marketing mindset?

A   To offer customers a comprehensive service catalogue
B   To offer competitively priced service offerings
C   To look at services from the customer's perspective
D   To utilise a wide range of communication channels

See Guide Chapter 2

SS 10

'Fitness for purpose' of a service comes from which of the following?

A The attributes of the service that have a positive effect on the performance of the business
B The ability of a service to remain operational at all times as agreed in an SLA
C The ability of a service to provide the required levels of functionality when required
D The service being provided by an outsourcing organisation

See Guide Chapter 2

SS 11

Which of the following is NOT an activity of Demand Management?

A Analysing and tracking business activities related to IT services
B Influencing demand for services using pricing incentives
C Redesigning business processes to match IT resource constraints
D Providing demand forecasts for capacity management

See Guide Chapter 8

SS 12

Which of the following are potential benefits of analysing patterns of business activity?

1 Service Design can optimise designs to suit business demand patterns
2 Financial Management can approve incentives to influence demand
3 Service Operation can adjust allocation of resources and scheduling
4 Service Portfolio Management can prioritise appropriate investments

A 1 and 3 only
B 2 and 3 only
C 1, 2 and 4 only
D All of the above

See Guide Chapter 8

SS 13

How is Financial Management applicable to the different types of service provider?

A   Financial Management is mostly applicable to external service providers
B   Financial Management is only applicable to Type II and Type III providers
C   Financial Management is less applicable for internal service providers
D   Financial Management is equally applicable to Type I, II and III service providers

See Guide Chapter 2
See Guide Chapter 7

SS 14

A goal of Financial Management is to ensure proper funding for the delivery of services. What is the main way in which this is achieved?

A   Introducing charging in order to generate required revenue and profit
B   Financial analysis and qualification of the future demand for IT services
C   Establishing mature accounting practices and procedures
D   Influencing demand for IT services to match current resources

See Guide Chapter 7

SS 15

Which of the following processes is NOT found within the Service Strategy publication?

A   Demand Management
B   Financial Management
C   Service Management
D   Service Portfolio Management

See Guide Chapter 2

ANSWERS TO 'SERVICE STRATEGY' QUESTIONS

SS 01
D The main purpose of the Service Strategy publication is to help organisations transform Service Management into a strategic asset. To operate and grow successfully in the long term, service providers must have the ability to think and act in a strategic manner. The Service Strategy publication provides guidance on how to develop such abilities.

SS 02
B All three statements are correct regarding the Service Portfolio. A Service Portfolio describes a provider's services in terms of business value and is used to manage the entire lifecycle of all services.

SS 03
C The Service Pipeline is a subset of the overall Service Portfolio and contains details of business requirements that have not yet become services released to the live environment. Option A refers to the Service Catalogue, Option B refers to the Service Portfolio, and Option D refers to Retired Services.

SS 04
B Statement 3 is incorrect. IT Governance does not enable process benchmarking. Benchmarking is a process in which organisations evaluate their processes in relation to best practice, usually within their own sector.

SS 05
B "A business case is a decision support and planning tool that projects the likely consequences of a business action."†

SS 06
A Option A refers more specifically to the financial analysis activity required to calculate Return on Investment as part of business case development.

SS 07
B Type I are internal service providers, Type II are shared service units, and Type III are external service providers.

SS 08
C "Value is defined not only strictly in terms of the customer's business outcomes. It is also highly dependent on the customer's perceptions. What the customer values is frequently different from what the IT organisation believes it provides. It is therefore essential for providers to demonstrate value, influence perceptions and respond to preferences."†

SS 09

C Rather than focusing inward on the production of services there is a need for providers to look at services from the 'outside in', from the customer's perspective. With a marketing mindset it is possible to understand the components of value from the customer's perspective, providing a deep insight into the challenges and opportunities related to the customer's business.

SS 10

A Fitness for purpose (utility) is the functionality offered by a product or service to meet a particular need. Options B and C both refer to 'warranty', which is 'fitness for use'. The warranty element in Option B is linked to the 'times as agreed in the SLA' and in Option C to 'when required'. Option D is not relevant to the question as utility can equally be provided by internal or outsourced service providers.

SS 11

C It is not an activity of Demand Management to redesign business processes to match IT resource constraints. Demand Management activities enable a service provider to understand and influence customer demand for services, and the provision of capacity to meet these demands.

SS 12

D All of the statements are potential benefits of analysing Patterns of Business Activity. Patterns of Business Activity (PBA) influence the demand pattern seen by service providers and PBA analysis provides input to the Service Management processes across the lifecycle.

SS 13

D Financial Management as a strategic tool is equally applicable to all three service provider types. Internal service providers are increasingly asked to operate with the same level of financial visibility and accountability as their business unit and external counterparts.

SS 14

B Option B relates directly to the financial planning required to secure proper funding for the delivery and consumption of services.

SS 15

C Service Management is not a process. The other three processes are all found within the Service Strategy publication. "Service Management is a set of specialised organisational capabilities for providing value to customers in the form of services."† ITIL has become the most widely accepted approach to IT Service Management in the world.

6 SERVICE DESIGN

The answers to questions in this chapter are on page 39.

SD 01

Which of the following most accurately identifies the two aspects of a Service Catalogue?

A   Operational Service Catalogue and Technical Service Catalogue
B   Operational Service Catalogue and Business Service Catalogue
C   Technical Service Catalogue and Business Service Catalogue
D   Internal Service Catalogue and Supplier Service Catalogue

See Guide Chapter 10

SD 02

Service Design relies on effective supplier and contract evaluation and selection. When selecting a supplier, which of the following should Supplier Management consider?

1   Track record
2   Capability
3   Credit rating
4   Size relative to the business being placed

A   1, 3 and 4 only
B   2 only
C   1 and 2 only
D   All of the above

See Guide Chapter 12

SD 03

Which of the following is NOT a process within the Service Design publication?

A   Service Portfolio Management
B   Service Catalogue Management
C   Service Level Management
D   Supplier Management

See Guide Chapter 3

SD 04

Which of the following statements are correct in respect of Service Design?

1   Service Design ensures not only that the functional elements of a service are addressed by the design, but also elements that facilitate management and operational performance
2   The main purpose of Service Design is the design of new or changed services
3   The goal of Service Design is to assist organisations seeking to plan the introduction of new or changed services and advise how to successfully deploy these new services into the production environment

A   1 and 2 only
B   1 and 3 only
C   2 and 3 only
D   All of the above

See Guide Chapter 3

SD 05

Which of the following statements regarding Maintainability is/are correct?

1   Maintainability is concerned with how quickly and effectively a service, a service component or an individual CI can be restored to its normal working status following a failure
2   Maintainability is the measure of how long a service or service component can perform its agreed function without interruption
3   Maintainability is a measure of compliance to a contract by a supplier

A   1 only
B   1 and 3 only
C   2 only
D   All of the above

See Guide Chapter 14

SD 06

A Service Design Package is a key concept in the design phase of the Service Lifecycle. Which of the following would you expect to find within a Service Design Package?

1   Organisational Readiness Assessment
2   Service contacts
3   Service functional requirements
4   Business requirements
5   Service Transition Plans

A   1, 3 and 4 only
B   5 and 3 only
C   2, 4 and 5 only
D   All of the above

See Guide Chapter 4

SD 07

The implementation of ITIL Service Management is about preparing and planning the effective and efficient use of which of the following?

A   People, Processes, Performance, Products
B   People, Processes, Products, Partners
C   Policies, Purpose, Projects, Practices
D   Planning, Price, Practicality, Performance

See Guide Chapter 3

SD 08

A customer-based SLA could be best described as?

A   A single agreement covering the needs of several customers
B   A single document that covers the differing needs of several customers
C   A multi-paged document that all parties agree complies with internal quality assurance requirements
D   A single agreement for an individual customer group that details the levels of service provided to that group

See Guide Chapter 11

SD 09

Which of the following is an alternative term used to describe a form of SLA Monitoring (SLAM) chart?

A RAG
B RACI
C ITAMM
D SMO

See Guide Chapter 11

SD 10

Which of the following is the best description of a document that details the initial requirements of the customer in terms of business needs?

A The Business Service Catalogue
B Service Level Requirements (SLR)
C Service Level Agreement (SLA)
D Service Overview Analysis (SOA)

See Guide Chapter 11

SD 11

Which of the following statements concerning SLAs is INCORRECT?

A SLAs are developed to match the business needs and expectations
B SLAs provide the basis for managing the relationship between the service provider and the customer
C SLAs are not required where there are no external customers
D SLAs define key service targets and responsibilities of the service provider and the customer

See Guide Chapter 11

SD 12

Which of the following should typically be considered when creating a Capacity Plan?

1   Cost forecasts for potential resources identified within the plan
2   A description of methods used to calculate potential capacity requirements
3   Detailed analysis on the cause of capacity related incidents
4   Improvement plans from Availability and Service Level Management

A   1, 2 and 3 only
B   1, 2 and 4 only
C   1, 3 and 4 only
D   2, 3 and 4 only

See Guide Chapter 11

SD 13

Availability Management needs to consider which two main elements?

A   Service and Component availability
B   Service and System availability
C   Hardware and Software availability
D   Component and System availability

See Guide Chapter 14

SD 14

Which of the following statements is/are correct?

1   The impact of a disaster may vary depending upon business conditions, when the disaster occurs, how long it takes to recover and the number of customers affected
2   However good an IT Service Continuity Plan is, it is impossible to completely eliminate all risks

A   1 only
B   2 only
C   Both of the above
D   Neither of the above

See Guide Chapter 15
See Guide Chapter 16

SD 15

When preparing which of the following documents would it be advisable to seek legal advice?

A   Service Catalogue
B   Service Level Agreement
C   Service Level Requirements
D   Underpinning Contract

See Guide Chapter 12

SD 16

To what does Single Point of Failure refer?

A   It is another term for 'mean time between failures' (MTBF)
B   A CI which, if it breaks, does NOT affect the availability of a service
C   A CI which, if it breaks, does affect the availability of a service
D   The Service Desk being a focal point for users and customers

See Guide Chapter 14

SD 17

Which of the following is NOT a goal of Service Design?

A   To design new and changed services for introduction into the live environment to satisfy business needs
B   To ensure a holistic approach to all aspects of Service Design is taken
C   To ensure there are efficient and effective processes for the design, transition, operation and improvement of services
D   To ensure that there is sufficient understanding of market spaces when analysing patterns of business activity

See Guide Chapter 3

SD 18

Supplier Management often has to comply with which of the following?

1   Internal corporate governance guidelines
2   External supplier purchasing requirements
3   Industry standard governance or legal requirements

A   1 only
B   All of the above
C   1 and 3 only
D   2 and 3 only

See Guide Chapter 12

SD 19

Which of the following is correct?

A   Service Level Agreements are written agreements between senior business representatives and external suppliers that document clearly what all parties are going to do for each other

B   Operational Level Agreements are written agreements between a service provider and another part of the same organisation

C   Operational Level Agreements are written agreements between Service Level Management and external service providers

D   Service Level Agreements is a term used by suppliers for Operational Level Agreements

See Guide Chapter 11

SD 20

The goal of Availability Management can best be described as?

A   To ensure that the level of service reliability delivered in all services is matched to the current and future agreed service levels negotiated with the Service Level Manager

B   To ensure that the level of service availability delivered in all services is matched to or exceeds the current and future agreed needs of the business, in a cost-effective manner

C   To ensure component availability is measured accurately and in a timely manner in order to fully understand overall end-to-end service availability achievements

D   To monitor performance of external service providers and suppliers to ensure they adequately underpin the overall needs of the user community as agreed in Service Level Agreements

See Guide Chapter 14

SD 21

Which of the following statements most accurately describes ITIL guidance regarding conducting Service Reviews?

A   Service Review meetings must always be held on a monthly basis

B   Periodic review meetings must be held on a regular basis with customers to review the service achievements in the previous period

C   Service Review meetings are always held with both the customer and external service suppliers and can be at any time to suit either party

D   Service Reviews must be held between Service Level Management and customer representatives only at the specific time agreed within the Service Level Agreement

See Guide Chapter 11

SD 22

Which of the following statements are correct in all cases?

1   Service Level Management produces reports on the progress and success of Service Improvement Plans (SIPs)
2   Service Level Management is responsible for the quality of services delivered to customers

A   1 only
B   2 only
C   Both of the above
D   Neither of the above

See Guide Chapter 11

SD 23

Which of the following statements is INCORRECT regarding Service Catalogue Management (SCM)?

A   SCM is responsible for ensuring agreed details of all services currently being provided, or those being prepared for transition to the live environment, are included in a Service Catalogue
B   SCM is responsible for ensuring customers are provided with informative data relating to the services being provided in the live environment, and that this information is current and relevant
C   SCM is responsible for ensuring details of all pipeline services are included in the Service Catalogue
D   SCM is responsible for ensuring service attributes, as agreed by the Service Level Manager and Service Portfolio Manager, are documented in the Service Catalogue and are kept under strict change control

See Guide Chapter 10

SD 24

Which of the following statements most accurately describes the overall goal of Information Security Management?

A   To protect the interests of customers and users by protecting systems from harm caused by failure of availability, confidentiality or integrity
B   To align IT security with business security requirements and to ensure that information security is effectively managed in all Service Management activities
C   To produce and maintain an overall Information Security Policy that defines the organisation's stance and attitude on all security matters
D   To develop an effective Information Security Management System that supports the business objectives and Information Security Policies

SD 25

Compliance to organisation-wide Information Security policy requirements should be referenced within which of the following documents?

1 Service Level Agreements
2 Operational Level Agreements
3 Third party underpinning contracts
4 Security policies

A 1, 3, and 4 only
B 1 and 4
C None of the above
D All of the above

See Guide Chapter 16

ANSWERS TO 'SERVICE DESIGN' QUESTIONS

SD 01
C   The correct terms for the two aspects of the Service Catalogue are the Business Service Catalogue and Technical Service Catalogue.

SD 02
D   All four factors should be considered. All four are relevant factors in evaluating and selecting a supplier who can deliver the service over a period of time to the required level. Each organisation should have clear processes and procedures for establishing new suppliers and contracts.

SD 03
A   Service Portfolio Management is included within the Service Strategy publication. The other three processes are included within the Service Design publication.

SD 04
A   The first two statements are correct in respect of Service Design. The third statement refers to the Release and Deployment Management process that is part of the Service Transition phase of the lifecycle.

SD 05
A   Maintainability is concerned with either preventing failures or enabling speedy recovery following a failure. Preventative maintenance will be carried out, for example, on hardware, to prevent failures from avoidable causes. Maintainability is often measured and reported as Mean Time to Restore Service (MTRS). Statement 2 refers to Reliability and statement 3 refers to Serviceability.

SD 06
D   The Service Design Package (SDP) details all aspects of a service and its requirements through all of the subsequent stages of the lifecycle. The SDP would therefore not only include the Service and Business Requirements but would also include a Service Transition Plan. A Service Design Package should be produced during the design stage, for each new service, major change to a service, or removal of a service.

SD 07
B   The implementation of ITIL Service Management is about preparing and planning for the effective and efficient use of the Four Ps (People, Processes, Products and Partners).

SD 08
D   A customer-based SLA is a single agreement for an individual customer group covering all SLM issues relevant to the particular customer group or business unit. Option A is discussing a service-based SLA and option B is describing a multi-level SLA. Option C is a generic statement. The customer-based SLA (option D) is where all the requirements of a customer are covered in a single agreement.

SD 09

A   RAG (Red, Amber, Green) is often used as an effective form of SLAM chart to visually display service performance. It provides an 'at-a-glance' overview, where Green is normal and in line with SLA targets, Amber would indicate a near breach, and Red would indicate there has been a breach of an SLA target.

SD 10

B   The SLR is the initial document around which the customer requirements for a service will be agreed and documented. Ultimately this will be the foundation for the SLA that is agreed. The SLR can be a difficult document to complete and requires considerable interaction between the customer and service provider to finalise.

SD 11

C   SLAs are required for internally provided services as well as those provided externally. All the other options are correct.

SD 12

B   When creating a Capacity Plan, the detailed analysis of the cause of capacity related incidents would not be considered. Any potential capacity requirements arising from capacity related incidents would have been managed at the time of the Incident and entered into an improvement plan (or, if the requirement was more urgent, would be processed via the Change process). Statements 1, 2 and 4 should be considered when creating a Capacity Plan.

SD 13

A   Availability Management is concerned with Service and Component availability. Availability Management needs to understand and manage both these interconnecting levels.

SD 14

C   Both statements are correct. The impact is always based on the impact on the business and therefore will vary depending on when the disaster happens. It is impossible to eliminate all risks; some are so large (e.g. tsunami) that there is no man-made elimination possible. Even where some action is possible to reduce risk, the costs of doing so may be prohibitive.

SD 15

D   It is advisable to seek legal advice when preparing an Underpinning Contract because it is a legal document. The other documents are internal and (on their own) carry no weight of law.

SD 16

C   A Single Point of Failure (SPOF) occurs in the situation where, if a CI fails, services relying on that CI will also fail. A SPOF represents an absence of Resilience.

SD 17

D Option D is not a goal of Service Design because it more specifically relates to activities within the Service Strategy phase of the lifecycle (i.e. defining the market, developing the offerings and managing demand).

SD 18

C There would be no requirement for Supplier Management to comply specifically with an external supplier's purchasing requirements. The Supplier Management process often has to comply with organisational or corporate standards, guidelines and requirements, particularly those of corporate legal, finance and purchasing as referenced in statements 1 and 3.

SD 19

B Option B correctly identifies OLAs as internal documents. Option A refers to external suppliers within an SLA which is incorrect. Option C also refers to contractual arrangements which is incorrect for an OLA. Option D is an incorrect statement.

SD 20

B This is the correct ITIL definition of the overall goal of Availability Management. It refers to Availability Management ensuring the service delivered is at a level that has been agreed with the business. Options A, C and D are elements of availability but discuss general aspects of the process rather than the overall goal. Option A is discussing Reliability, option C is discussing Measurement considerations and option D is discussing Serviceability and Supplier Management.

SD 21

B Service Reviews are held at a mutually agreed time but should be on a regular basis, in order to review performance achieved against performance agreed for the previous period. Options A and D are too specific, whilst option C is too open.

SD 22

C Both these statements are correct. SLM, in conjunction with CSI, will report on the progress of improvement actions contained within the SIP. SLM is responsible for ensuring the levels of service are as agreed in the SLA thereby providing a quality service.

SD 23

C SCM will not input details of any pipeline services into the Service Catalogue. The Service Catalogue will only contain services that are current or have been 'chartered'. Options A, B and D are correct.

SD 24

B Option B is the most accurate ITIL description of the goal of Information Security Management (ISM). The other options are important aspects of ISM but do not offer the most accurate description of the overall goal.

SD 25

D Information about Security Compliance requirements should be extensive and widely available to customers and users. It should be referenced in many different documents. The list, whilst not exhaustive, identifies typical documents where references to security policy matters would need to be made. The policies should be authorised by executive management within the business and IT. Compliance to the policies should be endorsed on a regular basis.

7 SERVICE TRANSITION

The answers to questions in this chapter are on page 52.

ST 01

Which of the following is NOT an objective of Release and Deployment Management?

A   To ensure there are comprehensive release and deployment plans
B   To ensure minimal unpredicted impact when deploying new services
C   To ensure all changes to services are reviewed in a controlled manner
D   To ensure releases are deployed efficiently and on schedule

See Guide Chapter 20

ST 02

The main goal of Knowledge Management is to enable organisations to?

A   Document all aspects of a new or changed service
B   Improve the quality of management decision making
C   Ensure compliance with data management legislation
D   Maintain accurate financial data regarding service assets

See Guide Chapter 17

ST 03

Which of the following is NOT a goal of Service Transition?

A   Setting customer expectations as to how the use of the changed service can enable business objectives to be met
B   Reducing variations in the expected and actual service performance of any service elements that are to be changed
C   Ensuring that secure and resilient IT infrastructures, environments, applications and data are designed for release into the live environment
D   Ensuring that the service can be used as it was intended

See Guide Chapter 4

ST 04

Which of the following statements regarding the Service Knowledge Management System (SKMS) is most accurate?

A   The main inputs to the SKMS are knowledge and wisdom
B   The SKMS monitors the knowledge management process
C   A Configuration Management System underpins the SKMS
D   A mature SKMS is essential for monitoring and reporting

See Guide Chapter 17

ST 05

Which of the following statements regarding CIs is INCORRECT?

A   A CI is an asset, service component or other item that is under the control of Configuration Management
B   CIs may vary widely in complexity, size and type
C   CIs may be grouped and managed together
D   A CI will have relationships with at least two attributes

See Guide Chapter 18

ST 06

What is the correct sequence for the following activities within the Normal Change process?

1   Create and record the RFC
2   Authorise and schedule the Change
3   Assess and evaluate the RFC
4   Review and close the Change record
5   Co-ordinate the Change implementation

A   1, 2, 3, 4, 5
B   2, 1, 3, 5, 4
C   1, 3, 5, 4, 2
D   1, 3, 2, 5, 4

See Guide Chapter 19

ST 07

From a Knowledge Management perspective, which of the following statements best describes Knowledge?

A   Education, formal qualifications and academic research
B   Discrete facts about services, events and activities
C   Experiences, ideas, insights and judgements of individuals
D   Tools and databases used to manage configuration data

See Guide Chapter 17

ST 08

Which of the following could typically be included within an SKMS?

1   Details about staff experience
2   Records of peripheral matters (e.g. weather, user numbers and behaviour)
3   Suppliers' and partners' requirements, abilities and expectations
4   Skills databases and professional development records

A   1, 2 and 3 only
B   2 and 4 only
C   All of the above
D   1 and 4 only

See Guide Chapter 17

ST 09

A secure storage facility where master copies of authorised software Configuration Items are stored could best be described as a ...?

A   Definitive Software Storage Library
B   Master Storage Library
C   Storage Area Network
D   Definitive Media Library

See Guide Chapter 18

ST 10

Which of the following are goals of Change Management?

1 To respond to customers' changing business requirements whilst maximising value, reducing Incidents, disruption and rework
2 To respond to business and IT requests for change that will align IT services with business needs
3 To minimise the number of quality and compliance issues caused by inaccurate recording of configurations and service assets

A 1 only
B 3 only
C 1 and 2 only
D All of the above

See Guide Chapter 19

ST 11

A change request could be described as a formal proposal for a Change to be made. Which of the following could be considered as change requests?

1 A request for change to a Service Portfolio
2 A request for change to a service or service definition
3 A project change proposal
4 A request to reboot a server

A 1 only
B All of the above
C 3 and 2 only
D 1, 2 and 3 only

See Guide Chapter 19

ST 12

How would you most accurately describe a change to a service for which the approach is pre-authorised?

A A Change Model
B A Standard Change
C A Usual Change
D A Normal Change

See Guide Chapter 19

ST 13

A Service Change could best be described as:

A   An authorised release or upgrade to an existing service that has successfully completed testing and is now scheduled for implementation

B   An architectural amendment to a configuration that could contribute to overall service performance

C   The addition, modification or removal of an authorised, planned or supported service or service component

D   A document from a customer that details the requirements for service amendments

See Guide Chapter 19

ST 14

Which of the following statements is correct regarding the Release Policy?

A   A Release Policy is always defined in the Service Strategy phase of the lifecycle to provide governance of the Release process and Release Management resources

B   A single Release Policy should be defined to govern all services and would include the expected frequency for each release type

C   A Release Policy should be defined for one or more services and would include the expected frequency for each type of release and the approach for accepting and grouping changes into a release

D   A Release Policy should always be renewed annually in line with financial planning cycles

See Guide Chapter 20

ST 15

Which of the following would normally be accepted as an Emergency Change?

A   A scheduled annual update to an accounting system

B   A release into a test environment to fix a program that is due to go live in two weeks time

C   A repair needed to restart the overnight batch processing after a failure

D   A request to change the functionality of a program

See Guide Chapter 19

ST 16

Which of the following statements about a Configuration Management System (CMS) is INCORRECT?

A A CMS is a collection of data that is stored together that describes aspects of a Configuration Item

B The CMS holds all the information required for CIs that are within the designated scope

C The CMS will be referenced for a wide variety of purposes during the Service Lifecycle

D The CMS typically contains configuration data and information that is combined into an integrated set of views for different stakeholders

See Guide Chapter 18

ST 17

Which of the following statements correctly describe how Service Transition adds value to the business?

1 Improving the ability to adapt quickly to new requirements and market developments thus providing a competitive edge

2 Improving the success rate of change and release implementations

3 Increasing confidence in the degree of compliance to business and governance requirements during implementations

A 2 only

B 2 and 3 only

C All of the above

D None of the above

See Guide Chapter 4

ST 18

What is the main purpose of the 'seven Rs' of Change Management within ITIL guidance?

A They represent the seven steps of the ITIL Change Management process

B They represent seven questions that must be considered when assessing a Change

C They represent the roles and responsibilities of staff involved in Change Management

D They are the seven tenets upon which Change Management depends

See Guide Chapter 19

ST 19

Why is remediation planning important in maintaining service availability?

A   To enable the customers to receive the correct level of utility thereby meeting availability targets
B   To enable financial management to make appropriate funding available to meet agreed availability targets
C   To enable Release and Deployment Management to implement approved changes according to the Release Policy
D   To enable services to be recovered with minimum negative impact on the business if a Change implementation fails

See Guide Chapter 19

ST 20

What is a Release Unit?

A   A part of the IT infrastructure that is unique in its composition
B   The portion of a service or IT infrastructure that is normally released together
C   A collection of authorised changes to the IT infrastructure
D   The document that identifies the schedule for different types of releases

See Guide Chapter 20

ST 21

The following statements are related to which ITIL concept?

- There is a defined trigger.
- The task is well known, documented and proven.
- Authority is effectively given in advance.
- Budgetary Approval will typically be preordained.
- The risk is low

A   A Configuration Model that is commonly used by all approved staff and users
B   A Standard Change
C   A repeatable Change Model that requires minimal interaction with change initiators or customers
D   A scheduled change review meeting

See Guide Chapter 19

ST 22

Which of the following are typically considered during remediation planning?

1 Back out plans
2 Baselines
3 Revisiting the original change request
4 Criteria for invoking Business/Service Continuity arrangements

A 1, 2 and 4 only
B 3 and 4 only
C 3 only
D All of the above

See Guide Chapter 19

ST 23

Which of the following may contribute to a Change Advisory Board meeting?

1 Change Manager
2 Customers
3 Facilities Manager
4 Suppliers and outsourcing partners
5 Representative from Financial Management

A 2, 3 and 4 only
B All of the above
C 1, 2 and 5 only
D 3, 4 and 5 only

See Guide Chapter 19

ST 24

Which of the following is NOT a purpose of Service Asset and Configuration Management (SACM)?

A To identify, control, record, audit, verify and provide reports on service assets and Configuration Items
B To account for, manage and protect the integrity of service assets and Configuration Items
C To ensure the integrity of assets contained in a Configuration Management System (CMS) and ensure the CMS is accurately maintained
D To improve asset management activities by ensuring changes to assets are appropriately authorised prior to implementation

See Guide Chapter 18

ST 25

Which of the following would NOT typically form part of the Definitive Media Library (DML)?

A Fire Safe
B Secure On-site Storage Facility
C Secure Off-site Storage Area Network
D User-controlled software libraries

See Guide Chapter 18

ANSWERS TO 'SERVICE TRANSITION' QUESTIONS

ST 01
C Ensuring changes are reviewed in a controlled manner is an objective of Change Management and not an objective of Release and Deployment Management.

ST 02
B The goal of Knowledge Management is to enable organisations to improve the quality of management decision making by ensuring that reliable and secure information and data is available throughout the Service Lifecycle.

ST 03
C Option C is a goal of Service Design. The Service Design Package details all aspects of the service and its requirements through all of the subsequent stages of the lifecycle. Options A, B and D all correctly refer to the goals of Service Transition.

ST 04
C Underpinning the SKMS will be a considerable quantity of data held in a central logical repository or CMS.

ST 05
D A CI does not have relationships with attributes. Attributes of CIs are recorded in the CMS and provide information about a CI. Options A, B and C are all correct.

ST 06
D Option D follows the correct sequence of activities within the ITIL Change Management process.

ST 07
C Knowledge is composed of the tacit experiences, ideas, insights, values and judgements of individuals. People gain knowledge both from their own and from peers' expertise, as well as from the analysis of information (and data). Through the synthesis of these elements, new knowledge is created.

ST 08
C A Service Knowledge Management System (SKMS) is a broader concept than the CMS and covers a much wider base of knowledge including, for example, staff experience, records of peripheral matters such as weather trends (think of how important this would be to insurance companies), user numbers, organisational performance and suppliers' and partners' requirements, abilities and expectations.

ST 09
D "The Definitive Media Library (DML) is a secure library in which the definitive, authorised versions of all media CIs are stored and protected. It may contain a variety of media such as tapes, CD-Roms, secure storage areas, along with associated documentation such as software licences etc."†

ST 10

C Statement 3 is a goal of Service Asset and Configuration Management, the other statements are goals of Change Management.

ST 11

B Change requests are raised for a wide variety of reasons and procedures should be in place to manage a range of different change requests, including those for minor or Standard Changes such as the example in statement 4.

ST 12

B A Standard Change is a Change to a service or infrastructure for which the approach is pre-authorised by Change Management and that has an accepted and established procedure. A Change Model would normally be associated with each Standard Change to ensure consistency of approach.

ST 13

C "A Service Change is correctly defined as the addition modification or removal of an authorised and supported service or service component and its associated documentation."†

ST 14

C Option C is correct. A Release Policy should be defined for one or more services and would include the expected frequency for each type of release and the approach for accepting and grouping changes into a release. Release and Deployment is primarily responsible for managing all aspects of the release process including the Release Policy.

ST 15

C An Emergency Change should only be accepted when the Change is intended to repair an error in an IT service that is negatively impacting the business to a high degree.

ST 16

A Option A refers to 'attributes' which provide information about individual CIs. Attributes of CIs are recorded in the CMS and provide information about a CI.

ST 17

C All of the statements correctly describe how Service Transition adds value to the business. Effective Service Transition can significantly improve a service provider's ability to successfully handle high volumes of changes and releases across its customer base.

ST 18

B The 'seven Rs' represent seven generic questions that must be answered when assessing a Change. They provide a good starting point in assessing and evaluating a Change. The 'seven Rs' are: Raised, Reason, Return, Risks, Resources, Responsible and Relationships. Without this information the impact assessment of a Change cannot be completed.

ST 19

D Remediation planning identifies how a service will be recovered to a known state after a failed Change or release. Effective remediation planning will reduce service disruption in the event of a failed Change and improve service availability. Ideally there will be a back-out plan. However, not all changes are reversible; in which case an alternative approach to remediation is required.

ST 20

B "A Release Unit describes the portion of a service or IT Infrastructure that is normally released together according to the organisation's Release Policy."† The general aim is to decide the most appropriate release unit level for each service asset or component.

ST 21

B A Standard Change is a pre-approved Change that is low risk, relatively common and follows an established procedure. The list of statements highlight common aspects of a Standard Change.

ST 22

D All four areas need to be considered during remediation planning. Remediation planning identifies how a service will be recovered to a known state after a failed Change or release. No Change should be approved without having explicitly addressed the question of what action will be taken if it is not successful. Ideally there will be a back-out plan. However, not all changes are reversible; in which case an alternative approach to remediation is required, possibly including revisiting the Change or invoking continuity options.

ST 23

B All could be contributors to a Change Advisory Board (CAB) meeting. The composition of the CAB is entirely dependent on the type of changes being considered. The CAB needs to include people with a clear understanding across the whole range of stakeholder needs, therefore, in reality, anybody could attend the CAB meeting, providing they have an interest or can add value to the meeting.

ST 24

D The authorisation of a Change to an asset would be the responsibility of Change Management. Options A, B and C all describe the purpose of Service Asset and Configuration Management.

ST 25

D Users could hold their own software libraries, however, they are unlikely to be secure or controlled adequately. Therefore user-controlled software libraries would not form part of the DML because they would not provide a 'secure and controlled environment'. The DML is a secure library in which the definitive, authorised versions of all media CIs are stored and protected. The DML is a single logical area even if there are multiple physical locations.

8   SERVICE OPERATION

The answers to questions in this chapter are on page 62.

SO 01

The ability for Service Operation to perform effective operational monitoring and control depends on data and information from which of the following processes?

A Incident Management
B Request Fulfilment
C Event Management
D Access Management

See Guide Chapter 26

SO 02

Which of the following statements regarding a Known Error are correct?

1 A Known Error should be raised when the diagnosis of a problem is complete and there is a workaround available
2 A Known Error can be raised as soon as it becomes useful to do so

A 1 only
B 2 only
C Both of the above
D Neither of the above

See Guide Chapter 24

SO 03

"A warning that a threshold has been reached, something has changed, or a failure has occurred"† describes which of the following?

A An Incident
B An Alert
C A Warning
D A Change

See Guide Chapter 26

SO 04

Which of the following is NOT a concept within the Access Management process?

A Identity
B Rights
C Access
D Possession

See Guide Chapter 16

SO 05

During the early stages of the Incident process the priority of the Incident is determined.

Which of the following statements regarding the initial priority is/are correct?

1 The initial priority of an Incident should not be changed once it has been assigned
2 The initial priority can be raised if a senior manager is adamant that it needs to be changed
3 If it appears that the Incident will not be resolved within the SLA target then the initial priority can be changed

A 1 only
B 2 and 3 only
C 3 only
D None of the above

See Guide Chapter 23

SO 06

In which of the following would the details of a workaround be documented?

A In a change proposal
B In the Technical Service Catalogue
C In a Problem record
D In an Event register

See Guide Chapter 24

SO 07

Which process would normally be used to efficiently handle low-risk, frequently occurring, low-cost small changes?

A   Incident Management
B   Request Fulfilment
C   Demand Management
D   Access Management

See Guide Chapter 5

SO 08

Which of the following is most significant in determining the priority of an Incident?

A   The impact on the business and how quickly the business needs a resolution
B   The seniority of the person logging the Incident
C   The ease and speed of implementing the fix
D   The ability of the Service Desk to rectify the Incident without referral to specialist support groups

See Guide Chapter 23

SO 09

An effective Request Fulfilment process can contribute to a reduction in workload for which two ITIL processes?

A   Change Management and Release & Deployment Management
B   Change Management and Problem Management
C   Change Management and Incident Management
D   Demand Management and Incident Management

See Guide Chapter 22

SO 10

Access Management will facilitate which of the following benefits?

1   Controlled access to services to enable an organisation to maintain the confidentiality of its information
2   Employees having the right level of access to execute their jobs effectively
3   An increase in the number of security breaches

A   1 and 2 only
B   1 and 3 only
C   2 and 3 only
D   All of the above

See Guide Chapter 16

SO 11

Event Management rely on which two types of monitoring tool?

A   Active and Passive
B   Upstream and Downstream
C   Owned and Leased
D   Manual and Automated

See Guide Chapter 26

SO 12

Which of the following is the best definition of a Problem?

A   An Incident that happens more than once
B   The unknown cause of one or more Incidents
C   An Incident that cannot be resolved
D   An Incident that has significant impact on the business

See Guide Chapter 24

SO 13

Which of the following processes will make most use of the Known Error Database (KEDB)?

A   Request Fulfilment and Incident Management
B   Incident Management and Problem Management
C   Access Management and Problem Management
D   Request Fulfilment and Access Management

See Guide Chapter 23
See Guide Chapter 24

SO 14

Which process has an objective "to provide a channel for users to request and receive standard services for which a predefined approval and qualification process exists"†?

A   Change Management
B   Request Fulfilment
C   Access Management
D   There are no ITIL processes with this objective

See Guide Chapter 19

SO 15

Which of the following describes a significant difference between a Service Request and an Incident?

A   An Incident always comes from a user, whereas a Service Request can originate from anyone in an organisation
B   A Service Request will sometimes be recorded by the Service Desk, whereas an Incident will always be recorded by the Service Desk
C   An Incident is unplanned, whereas a Service Request should usually be planned
D   A Service Request will never be escalated, whereas an Incident will always be escalated

See Guide Chapter 21

SO 16

Access Management executes policies and actions defined in which other Service Management processes?

A   Service Strategy and Service Design
B   Service Level Management and Request Fulfilment
C   Demand Management and Capacity Management
D   Availability Management and Information Security Management

SO 17

Which of the following is the main goal of the Incident Management process?

A   Restoring normal service as quickly as possible
B   Collecting all information relating to an Incident
C   Communicating with all interested parties
D   Ensuring that all Incidents are logged

See Guide Chapter 23

SO 18

Problem Management has two major areas of focus, what are they?

A   Reactive and intuitive
B   Reactive and proactive
C   Analysis and resolution
D   Identify and repair

See Guide Chapter 24

SO 19

Which of the following is NOT a recognised type of event described in ITIL?

A   Informational
B   Warning
C   Unusual
D   Exception

See Guide Chapter 26

SO 20

Which of the following would NOT normally be a trigger for the Access Management process?

A   A Problem
B   A Service Request
C   An RFC
D   A request from Human Resources (HR) Management

See Guide Chapter 16

SO 21

Which of the following statements correctly describe the purpose of Service Operation?

1   To deliver and manage services at levels agreed with the business
2   To manage the technology used to deliver and support agreed services

A   1 only
B   2 only
C   Both of the above
D   Neither of the above

See Guide Chapter 5

SO 22

Good communication is essential for effective Service Management. According to ITIL guidance, which of the following statements is INCORRECT?

A   Issues can often be prevented or mitigated with appropriate communication
B   All communication must have an intended purpose
C   Information should always be widely communicated
D   An organisation should have a communications policy

SO 23

With which other 'progressive' phases of the lifecycle does Service Operation need to interface?

A   Service Transition only
B   Service Design and Service Transition
C   Service Strategy, Service Design, Service Transition
D   Service Strategy, Service Design, Service Transition and CSI

SO 24

Which ITIL concept could be described as a "generic description for many varying types of demands that are placed upon the IT Department by the users"†?

A   Service Request
B   Standard Change
C   A customer requested event
D   Service demand

SO 25

'A server's memory utilisation is within 5% of its highest acceptable performance level.'

What would this typically be considered as?

A   An Incident
B   An Event
C   A Major Incident
D   A Problem

See Guide Chapter 26

ANSWERS TO 'SERVICE OPERATION' QUESTIONS

SO 01
C   "The ability to detect events, make sense of them and determine the appropriate control action"† is provided by Event Management. Event Management is therefore the basis for Operational Monitoring and Control.

SO 02
C   Both statements are correct. A Known Error is raised when the root cause of an Incident has been diagnosed and a workaround (permanent or temporary) has been identified. There may also be occasions when there is sufficient reason (benefit) to create a Known Error even if the exact cause is not known. In ITIL the phrase for this situation is 'as soon as it becomes useful'.

SO 03
B   This is the ITIL definition of an Alert. Alerts are managed by the Event Management process.

SO 04
D   Possession is not an ITIL concept within Access Management. Identity, Rights and Access are all ITIL Access Management concepts.

SO 05
B   It is incorrect to state that the initial priority of an Incident should not be changed. If the situation changes during the life of the Incident the priority can be changed to reflect the new conditions.

SO 06
C   During the Problem Management process, when a workaround is identified it should be documented in the Problem record. The Problem record would then remain accessible so that the details are available to staff who need the information, particularly Service Desk and Incident Management staff.

SO 07
B   Request Fulfilment would handle 'simple' changes and requests from users, wherever possible using Request Models.

SO 08
A   The priority of an Incident is normally based upon the 'Impact' (i.e. how much the business is being affected) and the 'Urgency' (how quickly the business needs a resolution).

SO 09
C   Request Fulfilment should reduce the number of changes needing to enter the Change process by taking care of 'small' changes. Without a Request Fulfilment process many Service Requests would need to be logged and managed as Incidents (e.g. request for advice or information).

SO 10
A An increase in the number of security breaches is not a benefit. Statements 1 and 2 correctly identify benefits of Access Management.

SO 11
A Active tools 'poll' or 'interrogate' CIs to check that they are operating normally. Passive tools are triggered into action by an event affecting the CIs and operate by 'informing' or 'notifying' the central event monitoring tool. The other options are all incorrect.

SO 12
B "A Problem is the unknown cause of one or more Incidents. The cause of the Problem is not usually known at the time a Problem record is created and the Problem Management process is responsible for further investigation."†

SO 13
B The KEDB is managed and used by Problem Management. Incident Management will also make frequent use of the KEDB in the resolution of Incidents related to Known Errors.

SO 14
B Option B, Request Fulfilment, correctly describes the objective.

SO 15
C A Service Request is usually something that can be, and should be, planned (e.g. moving a PC next week), whereas an Incident requires an immediate response as something 'unexpected' has happened. For option A, Incidents do not always come from users, they can come from other sources (e.g. monitoring tools). For option B, some Incidents may be recorded by other functions (e.g. IT Operations).

SO 16
D Access Management executes the policies and actions defined in Information Security and Availability Management. Access Management does not define the policies but executes actions based on the decisions made by Information Security Management and Availability Management.

SO 17
A 'Restoring normal service as soon as possible' is the main goal of Incident Management, remembering 'normal service' is as defined within the SLA.

SO 18
B Problem Management will mostly react to problems, however, in order to prevent reoccurrences of the same or similar problems it will be proactive. Proactive Problem Management activities also include analysing Incident records to identify trends and carrying out analysis to identify Problems that otherwise might have been missed.

SO 19

C   'Unusual' is not a recognised ITIL Event type. There are three recognised event types. The first 'Informational' identifies normal activity (e.g. transaction completed), the second 'Warning' identifies unusual activity (e.g. disk utilisation is approaching a threshold) and the third 'Exception' identifies 'abnormal' activity (e.g. server is down).

SO 20

A   A Problem would not normally trigger Access Management. (An Incident caused by a Problem may trigger Access Management.) The typical Access Management triggers would be a Service Request, an RFC or, in the case of option D, a specific form of Service Request from HR.

SO 21

C   Both statements correctly describe the purpose of Service Operation.

SO 22

C   It is incorrect to state that all information should be widely communicated. All communication should have an intended audience and a purpose; distribution therefore should be targeted to the intended audience.

SO 23

B   Service Operation is one of the three progressive lifecycle phases and needs to interface with the other two, Service Design and Service Transition. Value can only be realised in Service Operation if the Design is correct and the Transition into live Operation well managed. (Note: Service Operation will also interface with Service Strategy and CSI, the two 'ongoing' phases of the Service Lifecycle.)

SO 24

A   A Service Request is the ITIL concept to which the description refers.

SO 25

B   This would typically be considered an event, and in this particular case, because it is approaching a threshold, it would probably be a 'warning' event. The decision whether this would actually be a 'warning' or 'exception' event would be dependent on the organisation's definition of what is considered 'normal' operation.

9 FUNCTIONS

The answers to questions in this chapter are on page 67.

SF 01

Users report Incidents. Which of the following can also report Incidents?

1　Application Management staff
2　Technical Management staff
3　Service Desk staff
4　IT Operations staff
5　Network support staff

A　1 only
B　2, 4 and 5 only
C　1, 2, 4 and 5 only
D　All of the above

SF 02

Which of the following most accurately describes the main role of the Service Desk function?

A　To resolve all Incidents within SLA targets
B　To provide Incident data to Problem Management
C　To act as the 'single point of contact' for users and customers
D　To ensure all Service Requests are handled using Request Models

See Guide Chapter 21

SF 03

Which of the following statements is/are correct?

1   A Local Service Desk is close to the user community it serves
2   Use of Specialised Service Desk groups can allow faster resolution of specific types of Incidents
3   The use of a Virtual Service Desk is not recommended for large organisations

A   1 only
B   2 only
C   1 and 2 only
D   3 only

See Guide Chapter 21

SF 04

To which function does the following apply: '... the custodian of technical knowledge and expertise related to managing the IT Infrastructure'?

A   Application Management
B   IT Operations Management
C   Operations Control
D   Technical Management

SF 05

What are the two formal organisational structures within IT Operations Management?

A   IT Service Management and IT Operations Control
B   Computer Centre Management and IT Operations Support
C   Facilities Management and IT Operations Control
D   IT Operations Management and Facilities Management

See Guide Chapter 25

SF 06

Which of the following would NOT normally be recorded by the Service Desk?

A   Incidents
B   Service Requests
C   Standard Changes
D   Problems

See Guide Chapter 21

ANSWERS TO 'FUNCTIONS' QUESTIONS

SF 01

D Anyone may experience an Incident and call the Service Desk to report it. Users will report Incidents, technical staff may notice a failure, and tools can raise Incidents automatically.

SF 02

C The main role of the Service Desk function is to be the single point of contact for users and customers. An efficient Service Desk will contribute to higher levels of availability through participation in first line Incident Management.

SF 03

C Statements 1 and 2 are correct. Statement 3 is incorrect as a Virtual Service Desk can be an appropriate option for many large organisations.

SF 04

D This is a description of Technical Management. Technical Management refers to the groups, departments or teams that provide technical expertise and overall management of the IT Infrastructure.

SF 05

C The two formal organisational structures within IT Operations Management are IT Operations Control and Facilities Management.

SF 06

D Problems are recorded by Problem Management and would not normally be recorded by the Service Desk. The Service Desk will typically record Incidents, Service Requests and Standard Changes.

10 CONTINUAL SERVICE IMPROVEMENT

The answers to questions in this chapter are on page 72.

CSI 01

Which of the following is NOT an objective of Continual Service Improvement?

A Identifying, selecting and prioritising market opportunities
B Improving the cost-effectiveness of delivering IT services
C Making recommendations for improvements in each lifecycle phase
D Ensuring applicable quality management methods are employed

See Guide Chapter 6

CSI 02

"The primary purpose of Continual Service Improvement is to continually align and realign IT Services to changing business needs."† What is the main way in which this is achieved?

A Identifying and implementing improvements to measurement methods that support IT processes
B Identifying and implementing improvements to IT services that support business processes
C Identifying and implementing improvements to technologies that support IT processes
D Identifying and implementing improvements to business processes that support IT services

See Guide Chapter 6

CSI 03

What is the main goal of using the Deming Cycle?

A Measuring and reviewing improvements
B Facilitating steady ongoing improvement
C Performing an effective gap analysis
D Setting clear goals and targets

See Guide Chapter 31

CSI 04

Which are the missing steps from the CSI Model in the list below?

1 What is the vision?
2 Where are we now?
3 Where do we want to be?
4 How do we get there?
5 ?
6 ?

A 'Did we get there?' and 'Where should we go next?'
B 'How do we keep the momentum going?' and 'Did we get there?'
C 'What can we measure?' and 'Did we get there?'
D 'Did we get there?' and 'How do we keep the momentum going?'

See Guide Chapter 6

CSI 05

When improving processes, what are four important areas that measurements and metrics can be focused on?

A Purpose, Objectives, Inputs and Outputs
B Performance, Compliance, Quality and Value
C Objectives, Roles, Responsibilities, and Outcomes
D Performance, Resources, Measurability and Value

See Guide Chapter 30

CSI 06

Which of the following statements is correct?

A Baselines are a mechanism for real-time monitoring of quality
B Baselines need to be documented and accepted within an organisation
C Baselines must always be conducted by an independent third party
D Baselines are only used to validate earlier improvement activity

See Guide Chapter 30

CSI 07

Which of the following most accurately describes the relationship between technology and service metrics?

A   The main purpose of service metrics is to support technology metrics
B   Technology metrics are used in calculating end-to-end service metrics
C   Service metrics are not directly supported by technology metrics
D   Technology metrics are calculated from end-to-end service metrics

See Guide Chapter 30

CSI 08

Which of the following statements is INCORRECT in describing the role of a Service Owner?

A   The Service Owner provides a single point of accountability for their specific service
B   In complex, global organisations, Service Owners must always be full-time roles
C   Service Owners are primary stakeholders in the underlying processes which support their service
D   A Service Owner ensures that the Service Portfolio is accurate in relationship to their service

See Guide Chapter 11

CSI 09

In what order would you typically expect the following steps to be conducted when building a RACI matrix?

1   Conduct meetings and assign the RACI codes
2   Identify/define the roles
3   Distribute the chart and incorporate feedback
4   Identify the activities/processes
5   Identify any gaps or overlaps

A   1, 2, 4, 3 and 5
B   4, 5, 2, 1 and 3
C   2, 4, 1, 5 and 3
D   4, 2, 1, 5 and 3

CSI 10

Which of the following metrics would be LEAST useful in helping CSI identify opportunities for IT-related improvements?

A   Business metrics
B   Process metrics
C   Service metrics
D   Technology metrics

See Guide Chapter 30

ANSWERS TO 'CONTINUAL SERVICE IMPROVEMENT' QUESTIONS

CSI 01
A The guidance contained within the Service Strategy publication enables service providers to effectively identify, select and prioritise market opportunities. This is not an objective of Continual Service Improvement.

CSI 02
B Option B is focused on ensuring IT Services continually align to changing business needs. Whilst options A and C are valuable to CSI, the main way in which business alignment is achieved is through improving the IT Services that support the business processes. Option D is incorrect because IT services should support the business processes.

CSI 03
B The goal in using the Deming Cycle is steady ongoing improvement. The four key stages of the cycle are Plan, Do, Check, Act. Options C and D refer specifically to the 'Plan' stage, whilst Option A refers to the 'Check' stage.

CSI 04
D The missing steps from the CSI Model are 'Did we get there?' and 'How do we keep the momentum going?'. The CSI approach should verify that measurements and metrics are in place to ensure milestones are achieved, and ensure that momentum for quality improvement is maintained.

CSI 05
B Four key areas for process KPIs are Quality, Performance, Value and Compliance. Process metrics can help determine the overall health of a process and CSI would use these metrics as input in identifying improvement opportunities.

CSI 06
B It is very important that baselines are documented, recognised and accepted throughout the organisation. Baselines do not provide real-time monitoring, they do not always need to be conducted by an independent third party, and they are not only used to validate earlier improvement activity.

CSI 07
B Technology metrics, such as component- and application-based metrics are used to compute end-to-end service metrics.

CSI 08
B Service ownership is a critical Service Management role, although, as with many roles, this may or may not be a full-time position.

CSI 09

D Option D shows the typical order of steps to be conducted when building a RACI matrix. Defining the activities/processes, and the functional roles are the first two steps, followed by conducting a meeting and assigning the RACI codes. The RACI Matrix is a model used within organisations to effectively map the defined roles and activities of a process to existing staff.

CSI 10

A Business metrics would not typically be collected within Service Management as they would be the responsibility of business units outside IT. CSI focuses on IT service-related improvements, so business metrics will not be as helpful to CSI as the other metrics which will be used directly for identifying service improvements.

11 PROCESS

The answers to questions in this chapter are on page 76.

PR 01

Working with well-defined processes is a basic principle of ITIL. Which of the following statements most accurately describes a characteristic of a process?

A   A process delivers end-to-end monitoring of service quality
B   A process provides structure and stability for an organisation
C   A process utilises feedback for self-corrective action
D   A process ensures clear communication of service value

See Guide Chapter 1

PR 02

Which of the following statements best describes the value of process models?

A   To understand the future requirements for Service Management processes
B   To provide a logical model of the relationship between functions and processes
C   To understand the process and help articulate the distinctive features of a particular process
D   To report on the performance of process efficiency and effectiveness

PR 03

Which of the following is NOT a characteristic of a process?

A   The process should be traceable to a specific trigger
B   The outcome of a process must be automated
C   The specific result of the process must be identifiable
D   The performance of the process should be measurable

PR 04

Which of the following is LEAST important in ensuring processes are well managed?

A   Ensuring each process is owned by a Process Owner
B   Organising processes around a set of clear objectives
C   Aligning processes with international standards
D   Establishing process measurements and metrics

PR 05

Which of the following best describes the profile of a typical Process Owner?

A   Board-level executive with authority, leadership and charisma
B   External consultant with extensive ITIL qualifications and experience
C   Senior-level manager with credibility, influence and authority
D   Functional line manager with direct responsibility for operational teams

ANSWERS TO 'PROCESS' QUESTIONS

PR 01
C   Processes are examples of closed-loop systems because they utilise feedback for self-reinforcing and self-correcting action.

PR 02
C   When designing processes, process models help to articulate the distinctive features of a process and enable understanding of the various process elements (e.g. objectives, inputs, activities, outputs, roles, metrics etc.).

PR 03
B   It is not always possible or desirable to automate the outcome of a process and therefore it is incorrect to state that this is a characteristic of a process. Where possible, the automation of service processes can help improve the quality of service and reduce risk and cost.

PR 04
C   Aligning with international standards is the least important of the options listed in ensuring processes are well managed.

PR 05
C   A Process Owner should typically be a senior-level manager with credibility, influence and authority across the various areas impacted by the activities of the process. A Process Owner must be able to ensure compliance to the policies and procedures put in place across the cultural and departmental silos of the organisation.

12 TECHNOLOGY AND ARCHITECTURE

The answers to questions in this chapter are on page 79.

TA 01

Which of the following is NOT a potential benefit of automating service processes?

A   Reduced risk by reducing complexity
B   Improved quality of service
C   Increased variation in performance
D   Reduced cost of service

TA 02

Integrated Service Management technology should include certain core functionality. What would typically be added to the list below?

1   Integrated CMS
2   Workflow or process engine
3   Self-help
4   ?
5   ?
6   ?

A   Knowledge management, IT Governance, Quality System
B   Diagnostic utilities, Reporting, Dashboards
C   Online payment, Procurement, Accounting
D   Market analytics, Service Portfolio, Product Catalogue

TA 03

Integrated Service Management technology brings many benefits. Which of the following features would NOT directly benefit Incident Management?

A Integrated Configuration Management System
B Automated alerting and escalation
C Modelling and trend analysis
D Web interface to allow self-help

See Guide Chapter 23

TA 04

When selecting a support tool, what should be the first consideration?

A Is there sufficient budget to purchase and maintain the tool?
B Is the latest version of the tool available from the supplier?
C Is there a business benefit in buying the tool?
D Can the tool be integrated into existing Service Operation processes?

TA 05

Which of the following best describes a task for which a Service Management support tool would NOT be suitable?

A Very complex and variable tasks where there is a variety of inputs
B Simple repetitive activities
C Complicated repetitive activities
D Tasks that need to be carried out by a large number of people

ANSWERS TO 'TECHNOLOGY AND ARCHITECTURE' QUESTIONS

TA 01

C Increased variation in performance is not a benefit. When judiciously applied, the automation of service processes can help improve the quality of service, reduce costs and reduce risk through reducing complexity and uncertainty.

TA 02

B Integrated Service Management technology should provide certain core functionality including diagnostic utilities, reporting and dashboards.

TA 03

C Modelling and trend analysis would not usually be of primary interest to Incident Management. It would be more directly beneficial to other lifecycle processes such as Problem Management and Capacity Management.

TA 04

C There needs to be a clear business benefit for the purchase of any Service Management support tool. The justified statement of requirements is the starting point.

TA 05

A Service Management support tools are best deployed to automate repetitive and routine activities that are very similar each time they occur. Tools are typically not suitable to tasks where there are a wide variety of activities and inputs. Tools are most effective where there is a standard operating environment with clearly defined inputs and outputs.

13 SAMPLE QUESTIONS FROM ACROSS THE LIFECYCLE

The answers to questions in this chapter are on page 86.

To finish the book, here are some questions taken at random from across the Service Lifecycle.

A 01

A user calls the Service Desk to report that following the installation of a new version of the PC operating system their PC is running slowly.

After logging the call, what action should the Service Desk take?

A Refer it to Capacity Management because it could be evidence of a performance problem

B Process it as an Incident using the Incident Management process

C Refer it to the Change Manager because it may be that the Change was not implemented correctly

D Refer it to the Service Level Manager as it may cause a breach to the SLA

See Guide Chapter 21

A 02

Which of the following statements best reflects ITIL Guidance for Capacity Management?

A The Capacity Plan must be issued annually with quarterly reviews to ensure it remains accurate and reflects both current and future agreed capacity requirements

B The Capacity Plan should be issued each year in January so it coincides with the start of the budget year

C The Capacity Plan should be reissued every time there is significant change to the business or a new project is implemented

D The Capacity Plan should be prepared so it can be used as input into the organisation's budget process in line with the organisation's financial cycle

See Guide Chapter 19

A 03

Performance issues have been highlighted on a service and appropriate corrective improvements have been identified. Which ITIL process would authorise the implementation of these improvements?

A   Performance Management
B   Change Management
C   Capacity Management
D   Release and Deployment Management

A 04

The items in the following list are key aspects to be considered in which phase of the Service Lifecycle?

1   New or changed services
2   Service Management systems and tools
3   Technology architecture and management systems
4   The processes required
5   Measurement methods and metrics

A   Service Strategy
B   Service Design
C   Service Transition
D   Continual Service Improvement

See Guide Section 2

A 05

Which of the following benefits would be most quickly realised with the introduction of Service Level Management?

A   Significant improvements in service levels
B   Fewer calls to the Service Desk
C   The cost of IT services is reduced
D   Customer requirements are established

See Guide Chapter 11

A 06

What are the three basic elements of Financial Management?

A   Budgeting, IT Accounting, Charging
B   Budgeting, Forecasting, Charging
C   Budgeting, IT Accounting, Management Accounting
D   Costing, Charging, Management Accounting

See Guide Chapter 7

A 07

Which of the following would NOT be a consideration when deciding the appropriate level for release units?

A   The ease and amount of change necessary to release and deploy a release unit
B   The amount of resources and time needed to build, test, distribute and implement a release unit
C   The complexity of interfaces between the proposed unit and the rest of the services and IT infrastructure
D   The cost of the individual changes that are to be consolidated within the release unit

See Guide Chapter 20

A 08

Which phase of the Service Lifecycle will consider principles of design and methods for converting strategic objectives into portfolios of services and service assets?

A   Service Strategy
B   Service Design
C   Service Transition
D   Continual Service Improvement

See Guide Section 2

A 09

Which of the following statements about ITIL is INCORRECT?

A   It is a set of publications
B   It offers 'good practice' advice with room for self-optimisation
C   It is suitable only for medium to large organisations
D   It has been adopted worldwide

See Guide Chapter 1

A 10

An OLA is an agreement between an IT service provider and which of the following?

A   An external service provider
B   Another part of the same organisation
C   An internal customer
D   Both internal and external customers

See Guide Chapter 11

A 11

Which of the following statements most accurately describes the relationship between CSI and the Service Lifecycle processes?

A   CSI is predominantly dependent on the process within Service Operations
B   CSI interacts with the activities of all other Service Management processes across the lifecycle
C   CSI interfaces primarily with Service Strategy and Service Design processes
D   CSI is not dependent on any other Service Management process for improvement

See Guide Chapter 6

A 12

Which of the following is NOT a process within Service Operation?

A   Event Management
B   Request Fulfilment
C   Access Management
D   Application Management

See Guide Chapter 5

A 13

The Service Improvement Plan (SIP) is a key concept within CSI. Which other lifecycle process plays a significant role in creating and managing the SIP?

A   Availability Management
B   Service Level Management
C   Demand Management
D   Quality Management

A 14

Which of the following activities is NOT part of risk analysis?

A Evaluating possible vulnerabilities
B Deploying appropriate countermeasures
C Identifying current and future threats
D Identification of key IT Assets

See Guide Chapter 15

A 15

Which of the following activities would benefit from the availability of a Supplier and Contracts Database?

1 Supplier categorisation and maintenance
2 Negotiating terms to be included in new contracts
3 Evaluation and set up of new suppliers and contracts
4 Supplier performance management
5 Contract renewal and termination

A 1, 3 and 5 only
B 2 and 4 only
C 1, 3, 4 and 5 only
D All of the above

See Guide Chapter 12

A 16

When does an Incident become a Problem?

A When an Incident happens more than once
B When the impact of an Incident is greater than first anticipated
C When the reported Incident is considered to be a Major Incident
D Never

See Guide Chapter 23

A 17

The Deming Cycle does NOT contain which of the following steps?

A Plan
B Do
C Check
D Activate

See Guide Chapter 31

A 18

Which of the following are the five elements of an Information Security Management System (ISMS)?

A   Planning, Identification, Control, Status Accounting, Verification
B   Policy, Management System, Strategy, Controls, Risks
C   Control, Plan, Implement, Evaluate, Maintain
D   Threat, Effect, Incident, Damage, Control

See Guide Chapter 16

A 19

Which of the following is the best description of a Configuration Management System?

A   A set of tools, processes, procedures, policies and databases that are used to manage an IT service provider's configuration data
B   An Integrated Service Management tool that supports all the other processes and can be called upon by all stakeholders throughout the Service Lifecycle
C   A virtual tool that is owned and used by the SACM process owner
D   An integrated tool that highlights relationships between CIs

See Guide Chapter 18

A 20

Which of the following is responsible for keeping the user informed of the situation when there is a Major Incident?

A   The Service Desk
B   The Major Incident Manager
C   The Problem Manager
D   The Incident Manager

See Guide Chapter 23

ANSWERS TO 'SAMPLE QUESTIONS FROM ACROSS THE LIFECYCLE'

A 01
B All calls to the Service Desk need to be logged and then progressed as either an Incident or a Service Request. In this case the 'normal service operation' has not been achieved, therefore this is an Incident.

A 02
D Option D best reflects ITIL guidance. If the IT Capacity Plan is not prepared in time for the organisation's budget rounds, there will be no funding available to acquire resources leading to potentially serious shortfalls in service provision. Option A: ITIL is NOT prescriptive and does not give a timetable that has to be followed. In this example the suggestion of an annual plan with quarterly reviews is potentially appropriate for some organisations. Option B is again prescriptive and it would be too late to produce a Capacity Plan when budgets have already been agreed. Option C: ITIL advises that all changes, including changes originating from projects, should be assessed for the impact on Capacity, however, this will not, except in very special circumstances, result in the reissuing of the Capacity Plan.

A 03
B Change Management is responsible for approving (authorising) changes to controlled Configuration Items.

A 04
B The list details the five individual aspects of design considered within the Service Design publication. Covering all these areas during the design phase will ensure that there will be minimal issues arising during the subsequent stages of the lifecycle.

A 05
D The question asks for benefits of SLM that will be quickly realised. Options A, B and C may eventually happen, however, the SLM process will quickly identify customer requirements. A benefit of agreeing the 'real' customer requirement is to enable actions to be taken to tailor services to that requirement.

A 06
A The three elements of Financial Management are Budgeting, IT Accounting and Charging. Budgeting and IT Accounting are mandatory, whereas Charging is optional.

A 07
D When considering a release, decisions regarding costs will have been pre-decided via a business case or via Change Management (e.g. assessing cost in the CAB). Options A, B and C are all considerations that need to be taken into account when deciding Release Units.

A 08
B Service Design takes the objectives and requirements defined in Service Strategy and converts them into services and service assets. Service Design adopts a holistic approach to ensure all design aspects are considered and strategic objectives are realised.

A 09
C ITIL is suitable for all sizes and types of organisation, not only those that are of medium and large size.

A 10
B "An OLA is an internal agreement between the IT service provider and another part of the same organisation."†

A 11
B CSI interacts with the activities of all other Service Management processes. To support improvement activities it is important to integrate CSI within each lifecycle stage, including the underlying processes residing in each lifecycle phase.

A 12
D Application Management is in Service Operation, however, it is a function, not a process. Options A, B and C are all Service Operation processes.

A 13
B The SIP is a joint responsibility between CSI and Service Level Management. Availability Management will produce an Availability Plan which will feed into the SIP. Demand Management in Service Strategy also provides input into the SIP. Quality Management is not an ITIL lifecycle process.

A 14
B Deploying countermeasures is an aspect of Risk Management, not Risk Analysis. Risk Analysis is concerned with understanding assets that need to be protected, assessing the threats to those assets and then calculating the level of vulnerability (likelihood of occurrence) to the threats.

A 15
C Statements 1, 3, 4 and 5 can all directly benefit from a Supplier and Contract Database (SCD). The actual negotiation of terms within a specific contract is not facilitated by the SCD. The SCD provides a single source of information for the management of all suppliers and contracts.

A 16
D The Incident is the deviation from normal service operation, whereas the Problem is the underlying 'cause'. The Incident therefore never becomes the cause. A Problem Record results from a decision to investigate the cause of one or more Incidents, it is not 'automatic'.

A 17

D Activate is not a step within the Deming Cycle. The four stages of the Deming Cycle are Plan, Do, Check, Act.

A 18

C Option C correctly describes an ISMS. Option A highlights activities of SACM. Option B describes elements of the overall security framework. Option D is related to security controls.

There are five elements of an ISMS: Control (e.g. create a management framework for security); Plan (e.g. considering what the business needs are); Implement (e.g. ensure procedures, tools and controls are in place); Evaluate (e.g. audit for compliance and quality); and Maintain.

A 19

A Option A is the best description of the CMS. "The CMS is the set of tools and databases that are used to manage an IT service provider's configuration data. The CMS is maintained by SACM and is used by all other Service Management processes."†

A 20

A The Service Desk is responsible for all communication with users. All other processes will provide appropriate data and information to the Service Desk to enable communication to be timely and effective.

A NEW SERIES TO SUPPORT AN INDUSTRY
OF 25 MILLION PEOPLE

IT SERVICE MANAGEMENT
A Guide for Foundation
Exam Candidates

Ernest Brewster, Richard Griffiths,
Aidan Lawes, John Sansbury

October 2009

**IT SERVICE MANAGEMENT
FOUNDATION PRACTICE
QUESTIONS**
For ITIL®V3 Foundation
Exam Candidates

Steve Mann (Editor),
Tony Gannon, Nigel Mear

October 2009

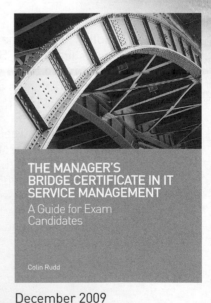

**THE MANAGER'S
BRIDGE CERTIFICATE IN IT
SERVICE MANAGEMENT**
A Guide for Exam
Candidates

Colin Rudd

December 2009

www.bcs.org/books

IT SERVICE MANAGEMENT
A Guide for Foundation Exam Candidates
ERNEST BREWSTER, RICHARD GRIFFITHS, AIDAN LAWES, JOHN SANSBURY

A fabulous new guide introduces ITIL both to Foundation Examination candidates and to professionals who require a practical understanding of IT Service Management.

The book is unique. It represents a very different approach in that the authors have used their collective experiences to help readers actually understand ITIL, not just memorise it. This will give candidates a winning edge in the exam because they will have the potential to work out the right answer, not just rely on a head full of facts and figures that will rapidly vanish. Service managers will develop an appreciation of the subject on which they can start to build expertise of real value to their organisations.

£24.95 200pp
ISBN 978-1-906124-19-9
Published: October 2009
www.bcs.org/books/itsmfoundation

'The no-nonsense approach of this book appeals to me. Straight-shooting description, examples and advice from experienced guys.'
Rob England - the IT Skeptic

IT SERVICE MANAGEMENT FOUNDATION PRACTICE QUESTIONS
For Foundation Exam Candidates
STEVE MANN, TONY GANNON AND NIGEL MEAR

The most authoritative guide to preparing for the ITIL Foundation Certificate in IT Service Management. It includes an extensive range of practice questions complete with explanations and key learning points and will greatly assist anyone sitting or intending to sit the V3 ITIL Service Management Foundation Certificate. It provides a wealth of background knowledge and sample questions using different styles with detailed explanations that are intended to build on existing study or learning. This guide utilises the experience of three established independent service management consultants who are members of the ISEB examination panel and are experienced service management trainers.

'Well written, concise, practical advice for students on how to approach multiple choice examination questions. Puts into words what the experienced tutor has been saying for years. Well done.'
Dave Jones - Pink Elephant

£24.95 100pp
ISBN 978-1-906124-18-2
Published: October 2009
www.bcs.org/books/itsmquestions

THE MANAGER'S BRIDGE CERTIFICATE IN IT SERVICE MANAGEMENT
A Guide for Exam Candidates
COLIN RUDD

The Manager's Bridge Certificate is intended for those who have an ITIL Manager's Certificate in IT Service Management and wish to bridge the gap between their existing qualification and 'ITIL Expert in IT Service Management'.

The main focus of the Manager's Bridge is the new content of ITIL V3 and the content that has changed. The book is closely aligned to the structure of the syllabus. It can either be used as a learning aid for self study or as a reference or revision aid within an accredited training course.

Colin Rudd has worked in the IT industry for over 35 years and has been heavily involved in the development of the IT Infrastructure Library (ITIL). He is former president of the Institute of IT Service Management and is currently a director of itSMF International and Chair of the itSMF Standards Management Board.

£29.95 150pp
ISBN 978-1-906124-20-5
Published: December 2009
www.bcs.org/books/managersbridge

BUSINESS ANALYSIS TECHNIQUES
77 Essential Tools for Success
JAMES CADLE, DEBRA PAUL AND PAUL TURNER

Business analysts are generally charged with the investigation of ideas and problems. Their role is to formulate options for a way forward and produce business cases setting out conclusions and recommendations. The development of business analysis as a professional discipline has extended the role of the business analyst who now needs the widest possible array of tools. This book provides 77 possible techniques and applies them within a framework of stages such as 'Investigate Situation', 'Define Requirements' and 'Manage Change'.

The book complements Business Analysis (ed Debra Paul and Donald Yeates) published by BCS. The book will be of enormous benefit to practising business analysts and to managers in any area requiring a comprehensive single source of practical advice on the use of business analysis techniques. It will also be of considerable interest to students of information systems and business strategy.

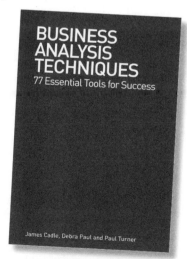

£29.95 250pp
ISBN 978-1-906124-23-6
Published: February 2010
www.bcs.org/books/batechniques